Shark Attack!

Gail Tuchman

SCHOLASTIC INC.

New York Toronto London Auckland
Sydney Mexico City New Delhi Hong Kong

Read more! Do more!

Download your free all-new digital book,
Shark Attack! Reading Fun

Quizzes to test your knowledge and reading skills

Fun activities to share what you've discovered

Log on to
www.scholastic.com/discovermore/readers
Enter this special code: L2DMFXD774P2

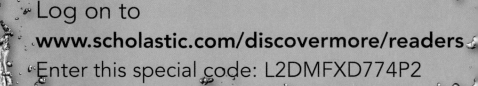

Contents

EDUCATIONAL BOARD:
Monique Datta, EdD, Asst. Professor, Rossier School of Education, USC;
Karyn Saxon, PhD, Elementary Curriculum Coordinator, Wayland, MA;
Francie Alexander, Chief Academic Officer, Scholastic Inc.

ISBN (Trade) 978-0-545-53377-5
ISBN (Clubs) 978-0-545-62401-5

12 11 10 9 8 7 6 5 4 3 2 1   13 14 15 16 17 18/0

Printed in the U.S.A.   40
This edition first printing, August 2013

Scalloped hammerhead shark

Ocean hunters

Basking shark

Bull shark

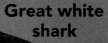

Great white shark

The shortfin mako is hunting. It speeds toward its prey at 20 miles per hour. Its huge mouth is open and ready. Sharks are the great hunters of our oceans. The shortfin mako is the fastest shark of all.

Oceanic whitetip shark

Leopard shark

4

Tiger shark

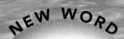

NEW WORD

prey

pray

An animal that is **prey** is hunted down and may be killed by another animal.

SAY IT OUT LOUD

Caribbean reef sharks

Silky shark

Shortfin mako shark

5

Here are more supercool sharks.
Sharks are fish. The whale shark is the
biggest shark. It's the world's biggest
fish. It can grow to 40 feet long.

How big am I?   Dwarf
                lanternshark   Human

The 7-inch dwarf lanternshark fits into a person's hand. Its belly glows. It can't be seen from below. This hides the shark from animals that want to eat it!

This is the smallest shark in the ocean.

This is the biggest shark in the ocean.

Whale shark

T. rex

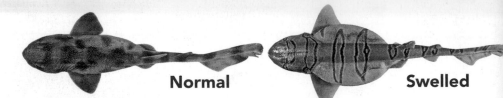

Normal   **Swelled**

The swell shark has a secret.
It can swallow lots of water and
swell up to twice its size. Now it's
hard for another animal to bite it.

The shortfin mako can leap
20 feet out of the water!

420 million years ago

Sharks are living
in the ocean.

200 mya

Dinosaurs rule
the planet.

Sharks are survivors. They've been swimming in our waters for more than 400 million years. Sharks were here long before dinosaurs ruled the planet.

Ancient sharks ate dinosaurs that fell into the sea!

60 mya

Mammals thrive.

190,000 years ago

Humans are living in Africa.

Amazing bodies

Why have sharks survived so long? Their amazing bodies make them the best hunters in the ocean. A shark's skeleton is made of cartilage. Cartilage bends more easily than bone does. It helps the shark twist and turn in the water.

Great white shark

It's a fact!

A shark takes in water to breathe. The water leaves the body through the gill slits.

Sharks never run out of teeth.

Fins help a shark move forward, balance, and steer.

Denticles are rough scales that protect a shark's body.

Teeth are the bony parts of a shark. A shark can use 30,000 teeth in its life.

NEW WORD

cartilage

KAHR-tuh-lij

Your ears and nose are formed by strong, rubbery **cartilage**.

SAY IT OUT LOUD

If a tooth falls out, a new one moves in.

You have five senses.
Sharks have six super senses
to track down their prey.

Hearing Sharks hear
sounds too low for
you to hear.

Taste Your taste buds
are mostly on your tongue.
Sharks' taste buds line their
mouths and throats.

Some sharks can smell blood up to 3 miles away.

Nurse shark

Smell You use your nose to smell and breathe. Sharks use theirs for smelling prey.

A great white takes a test bite. It tastes to find out if its prey is good to eat.

13

Sight
Sharks can see about ten times better in low light than you can.

The blue shark has a special layer in its eye for seeing in the dark sea.

Touch
You feel things when you touch them. Sharks feel vibrations from things *before* they touch them.

Electroreception

Sharks have a sixth sense. They sense electricity in other animals. This helps them find out where dinner is hiding!

These pores can sense electricity.

Scalloped hammerhead shark

Eat up!

A shark's main job is feeding. Sharks rarely attack humans to eat them. People are bony and don't taste good. Sharks eat fish and other smaller ocean animals. They even eat other sharks!

Old boot

Stingray

Squid

Plankton

A tiger shark
will eat anything—
even a boot!

The nurse shark traps
and sucks up squid.

The hammerhead
shark likes stingrays
best of all.

The giant whale shark
eats tiny plankton—
tons of it!

17

A great
white shark
tracks a seal.
The seal is rich
in fat. The shark
swims fast, near the
top of the water. It's now
a few feet from the seal.
The great white points its
snout upward. It bursts out
of the water with its jaws open
wide. It pushes its upper jaw and
teeth forward. Its teeth find their
mark. *Chomp!*

It's a fact!

After eating a baby seal, a great white

can survive 12–15 days without feeding.

A horn shark scents an egg case. It bites with strong jaws and flat back teeth—*crunch!*

Slurp! A cookie-cutter shark attaches its lips to prey. It bites using pointy, razor-sharp teeth. The shark cuts out a bite as round as a cookie!

A basking shark glides through the sea. Its mouth is open. It collects water, and strains out plankton with its gill rakers.

NEW WORD

plankton
PLANGK-tuhn
Tiny animals drifting in the ocean are **plankton**.

SAY IT OUT LOUD

Coral reefs teem with ocean life. One in four kinds of all ocean animals are found here.

Whitetip reef shark

Coral reefs are made from the skeletons of billions of tiny sea creatures.

Sharks rule coral reefs. They keep reefs healthy by eating weak and sick animals.

Blacktip reef shark

Shark attacks

People are more likely to be killed by sharks in Australia than in any other place. But the number of attacks is small.

5

3
COCOS
ISLANDS

AUSTRALIA

WESTERN
AUSTRALIA

65

Around the world, crocodiles, dogs, and pigs each kill more people every year than sharks do. People are a much bigger danger to sharks than sharks are to people.

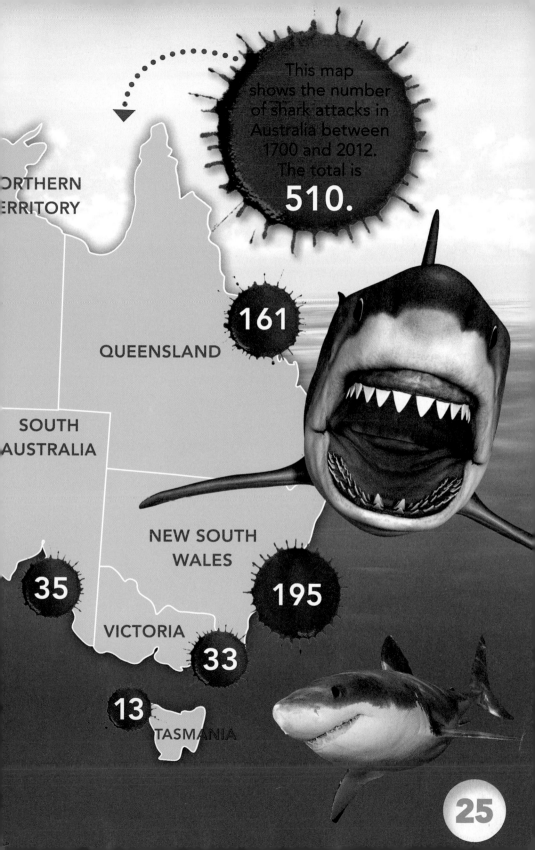

This map shows the number of shark attacks in Australia between 1700 and 2012. The total is **510.**

NORTHERN TERRITORY

QUEENSLAND 161

SOUTH AUSTRALIA

NEW SOUTH WALES 195

35

VICTORIA 33

13 **TASMANIA**

Sharks under attack

Humans are sharks' main predators. As many as 100 million sharks are killed by people every year.

Shark fins are used to make shark fin soup.

Many sharks are caught in nets set for other fish.

Dr. Ellen K. Pikitch is a scientist and "shark hugger." She says:

"Sharks are sensitive creatures. They need our help. They must not be killed in the numbers they are now. One way to help them is to create safe areas where they won't be hunted. We must work to get the word out about the dangers sharks face."

NEW WORD

predator

PRED-uh-tur

A **predator** hunts down and may kill another animal.

SAY IT OUT LOUD

World of sharks

We humans find sharks to be both terrifying and beautiful. There are more than 400 kinds of sharks in our seas. They are unlike any other animals on Earth. Let's help

Blue sharks feed on a school of anchovies in the warm waters off California.

them survive. Let's keep the seas swimming with supercool sharks. Their future depends on our respect for them and their watery world.

Glossary

anchovy
A small ocean fish that may be salted and canned for people to eat.

cartilage
A strong, flexible material that forms a shark's skeleton.

denticle
A rough scale that helps protect a shark's body.

electroreception
The sense system that sharks use to detect electric signals given off by other animals.

fin
A stiff part on a shark that moves it forward through the water or helps it balance or steer.

gill raker
A body part in certain sharks that catches and strains food from the water.

gill slit
An opening on a fish's body out of which water passes after the fish has used it to breathe.

plankton
Tiny animals and plants that drift or float in oceans or lakes.

predator
An animal that hunts other animals for food.

prey
An animal that is hunted by another animal for food.

reef
A strip of rock, sand, or coral just below the surface of a body of water.

scale
A thin, flat piece of hard skin on a fish's body.

sensitive
Affected even by very small changes.

skeleton
The set of bones that supports and protects the bodies of some animals.

steer
To make something go in a particular direction.

survivor
Someone or something that lives for a long time or through hard times.

swallow
To make food or drink move from the mouth to the stomach.

teem
To be very full of.

thrive
To be healthy and strong.

vibration
A fast movement back and forth.

Index

Image credits

Photography and artwork
1: Andy Murch/Visuals Unlimited; 2cl: Andreas Meyer/Shutterstock; 2–3b (water): Irochka/Fotolia; 3: Rob Stegman/iStockphoto; 4–5 (background): Nastco/iStockphoto; 4tl: Andy Murch/Visuals Unlimited; 4tc: Chris Dascher/iStockphoto; 4cl: Fiona Ayerst/iStockphoto; 4bl: Chris Dascher/iStockphoto; 4br: Reinhard Dirscherl/Visuals Unlimited; 4bc, 5l: Andy Murch/Visuals Unlimited; 5tc: Amanda Cotton/iStockphoto; 5crt, 5crm: Chris Dascher/iStockphoto; 5crb: Kadri Ates Evirgen/iStockphoto; 6–7 (main image): Alexis Rosenfeld/Science Photo Library/Science Source; 6 (human icon): Tulay Over/iStockphoto; 6–7 (whale shark icon): Scholastic Inc.; 7 (hand): peshkova/Fotolia, 7 (lanternshark): Seapics.com; 7 (dinosaur icon): Pro Web Design/Fotolia; 8t: T. Carter/Science Image/CSIRO; 8c: Mandy Hague; 9: Jon Hughes, jfhdigital.com; 10–11 (main image): Michael Patrick O'Neill/Science Photo Library/Science Source; 10bl: NatalyArt/Fotolia; 10bc: Alexis Rosenfeld/Science Photo Library/Science Source; 11tl: iLexx/iStockphoto; 11tr: Eye of Science/Science Source; 11br: BW Folsom/Shutterstock; 12cl: ia_64/Fotolia; 12cr: Scholastic Inc.; 12–13b: Mark Conlin/Alamy Images; 13 (blood): stockcam/iStockphoto; 13tr: Stephen Frink/Corbis Images; 14t: Masa Ushioda/Media Bakery; 14cr: gosphotodesign/Fotolia; 14b: Scholastic Inc.; 15cr: Doug Perrine/Nature Picture Library; 15b: iStockphoto/Thinkstock; 16 (t to b): Julian Rovagnati/Shutterstock, Cor Bosman/iStockphoto, bernd.neeser/Shutterstock, bluehand/Shutterstock; 17 (t to b): Albert kok/Wikipedia, Stephen Frink/Corbis Images, Seapics.com, Martin Strmiska/Alamy Images; 18–19 (t, b): Scholastic Inc.; 18–19 (main image): Fabrice Bettex/Alamy Images; 20tl: Marine Themes; 20b: Dan Burton/Nature Picture Library; 20–21b (various plankton): bluehand/Shutterstock, micro_photo/iStockphoto, digitalbalance/Fotolia; 21tr: Seapics.com; 21b: Louise Murray/Science Source; 22–23 (background): Tobias Helbig/iStockphoto, 22 (shark): David Fleetham/Visuals Unlimited; 22 (yellow fish): Richard Carey/iStockphoto; 22 (coral bl): microgen/iStockphoto; 22 (shrimp): rep0rter/iStockphoto; 22 (eel): Richard Carey/iStockphoto; 22–23 (coral bc): Dirk-Jan Mattaar/iStockphoto; 23 (sharks): R. Gino Santa Maria/Shutterstock; 23 (turtle): Zoonar/Thinkstock, 23 (yellow fish): Predrag Vuckovic/iStockphoto; 23 (clownfish br): marrio31/iStockphoto; 24–25 (background): iLexx/iStockphoto; 24–25 (map): Arunas Gabalis/Shutterstock 24cl: Chris Dascher/iStockphoto; 25cr: Andreas Meyer/Shutterstock; 25br: Michae Patrick O'Neill/Science Source; 26–27t (blood): Scholastic Inc.; 26–27 (main image Brian Skerry/National Geographic/Getty Images; 26 (bowl): studyoritim/iStockphoto; 26 (spoon): Scholastic Inc.; 27 (paper): Electric_Crayon/iStockphoto; 27 (tape): spxChrome/iStockphoto; 27 (photo frame): kevin llewellyn/iStockphoto 27 (diver with shark): Institute for Ocean Conservation Science/Stony Brook University; 28–29: Seapics.com; 30–31: Chris Fallows/www.apexpredators.com.

Cover
Front cover: (icon) Jan Dabrowski/iStockphoto; (main image) Alexander Safonov/Getty Images; (bc) cameilia/Shutterstock; (br) Katseyephoto/Dreamstime.
Back cover: (computer monitor) Manaemedia/Dreamstime. Inside front cover: (all) Scholastic Inc.

Thank you

For their generosity of time in sharing their expertise, special thanks to: George H. Burgess, Director of the Florida Program for Shark Research and Curator of the International Shark Attack File, Florida Museum of Natura History; Dr. Ellen K. Pikitch, marine biologist and Executiv Director of the Institute for Ocean Conservation Science, Stony Brook University School of Marine and Atmospheri Sciences; Drury Thorp, cofounder of Shark Savers; Kim Dennis-Bryan, for expert consultation; and Mike Coots, for sharing his passion. Shark attack data on pages 24–25 © International Shark Attack File, Florida Museum of Natural History, University of Florida.